# EPPING and ONGAR
## A Pictorial History

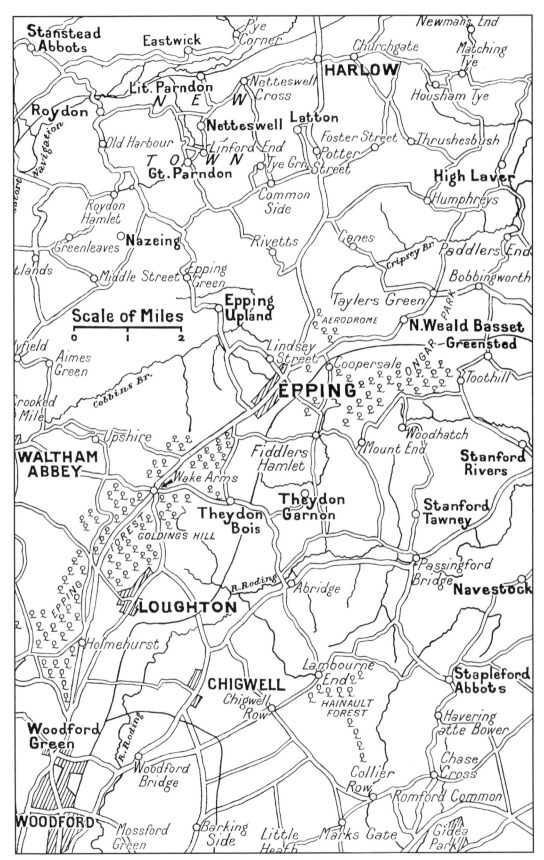

General map of the Epping area.

# EPPING AND ONGAR
## A Pictorial History

**Stephen Pewsey**

**Phillimore**

1997

Published by
PHILLIMORE & CO. LTD.
Shopwyke Manor Barn, Chichester, West Sussex

ISBN 1 86077 060 6

Printed and bound in Great Britain by
BIDDLES LTD.
Guildford, Surrey

*This book is for Ellen Rose*

# List of Illustrations

*Frontispiece:* Map of the Epping district

# *Acknowledgements*

I am grateful for the suggestions and support from many people in the Epping Forest area in producing this book. The staff at Epping Forest District Museum were most generous with their time and advice and without their help this book would not have been possible. In particular, I would like to thank David Hodges, whose help was invaluable, the Curator, Sue Davies, who was kind enough to expedite the whole project, and Rosie Wade, who guided me through the museum's superb photographic archive. I would also like to thank my wife Paulette for her support and technical assistance, and Brian Page for tracing some of the postcards used in this volume.

For permission to use many of the photographs, I would like in particular to thank Epping Forest District Museum, who have been most generous in allowing me to reproduce many of their copyright images. Other images are reproduced courtesy of The British Library, Essex County Libraries, Jack Farmer Esq., Mrs. May Clark, and the Eclipse Archive. Some of the line drawings and a few of the photographs have been reproduced from early issues of the *Transactions of the Essex Archaeological Society*, the *Essex Review*, and other books from the author's own collection.

# Introduction

The area covered by this book is the former Rural District of Epping and Ongar, which, before the local government reorganisation of 1974, stretched over a broad swathe of south-west Essex focusing on the two very different towns of Epping and Ongar. Within this large area, which stretches from the edge of the metropolis almost to the heart of Essex, there is a fascinating and disparate heritage. The stamp of the landscape is unmistakable on human activity in the district, but it is landscape of great variety. To the west, hornbeam, oak and lime have held sway since the Ice Age on the high ridge we now call Epping Forest, while in the heart of the area the young River Roding winds lazily. Fertile farmlands predominate to east and north, the rolling landscape dotted with villages which are typically polyfocal, that is, comprising several 'ends' rather than a single settlement.

Human settlement in the area goes back at least to the Ice Age; it was the glaciers of the Ice Age which spread the broad belt of boulder clay across central Essex, making it a fertile terrain, in contrast with the more barren pebbly soils along the Epping Forest ridge. As early as the Mesolithic period, in about 7,500 B.C., roving bands of hunter-gatherers passed through the area, leaving traces of a temporary camp at High Beach, where their abandoned flint-knapping site was discovered early this century. There are scattered traces of Neolithic and Bronze-Age activity too, notably at Fyfield and Navestock, where 'founder's hoards'—kits of scrap bronze and completed objects—form part of a line of such hoards stretching from what is now Cambridge to the Thames. This was supposedly a bronze-smiths' trail, with 'dumps' of bronze ready for working placed at regular strategic intervals.

By the Iron Age (*c*.650 B.C. - A.D. 43) settlement in the area was widespread and we begin to see hints of political organisation. The Essex landscape becomes dotted with massive earthen forts, with impressive systems of ditches and embankments. In our own area are the forts of Ambresbury and Loughton Camp. These defensive strongholds are very close together, and it has been suggested that one replaced the other. However, local archaeologist Peter Huggins has recently pointed out that there are several similar examples across Essex, and that in all cases the two forts face each other across boundaries of the old hundreds. Hundreds are Anglo-Saxon administrative divisions, but they could easily be based on much older blocs of land. Ambresbury Banks is just inside Waltham Hundred, while Loughton Camp is on the border of Ongar Hundred. It has been argued that the eight (formerly nine) parishes of The Rodings similarly form a cohesive territory whose boundaries pre-date the Roman occupation.

At the time of the Roman occupation, the Epping and Ongar area lay in the tribal state of the Trinovantes. The Roman road from London to Great Dunmow neatly cuts the area in two; the village of Moreton is actually built on top of the road. There is little evidence, however, of any major Roman settlement in the district. The river-crossing at Passingford Bridge has been suggested as the site of the 'lost' Roman town of *Durolitum*, though Chigwell and Romford have also been proposed. There may have been a villa at Ongar, but the area seems to have been mainly rural and no doubt well-wooded.

In this agricultural landscape, the transition from Roman to Saxon rule may have been relatively peaceful. Place-names in the area are overwhelmingly Anglo-Saxon; -*ingas* place-names such as Epping and The Rodings are thought to indicate a secondary wave of settlement after the first, mainly coastal, invasions. There is little archaeological evidence for early Anglo-Saxons, apart from some weaving activity shown by a loom-weight found at Blackmore. The area may have been a rural backwater in both Roman and Saxon periods, though the Saxon name of Loughton Camp, *sateres byrig*, or 'robbers' camp', gives a hint of darker goings-on.

The place-name Epping means 'upland settlers', while Ongar simply means 'grass-land'. Anglo-Saxon place-names generally refer either to some feature in the landscape (Lambourne = 'muddy stream') or to some important settler (Bobbingworth = 'the enclosure of Bubba's people').

Most of the area covered by this book formed part of Ongar Hundred in Anglo-Saxon times; the origins of these divisions are lost in the mists of antiquity, but hundreds were essentially for the administration of justice, calling out the militia, and circulating news and information. Each hundred had a central meeting place, and Ongar's may have been at Ongar itself or, more probably, at Toot Hill.

The Norman Conquest in 1066 saw a major change of landowners throughout Essex as followers of King William were rewarded for their loyalty. The Domesday Survey of 1086 gives a good picture of conditions at the time. Count Eustace of Boulogne held Ongar, while Epping was owned by the canons of Waltham Abbey. The Normans left a considerable legacy, social as well as architectural. Many churches in the Epping and Ongar area were built or rebuilt in stone by pious Norman landowners, while their names are recorded in the landscape. Norton Mandeville, a reminder of the Mandeville family who were once earls of Essex; the Tany family in Stapleford Tawney, the Gernons in Theydon Garnon.

In the high Middle Ages the area seems to have prospered, despite the vagaries of famine and disease. The original focus of settlement at Epping had been along Epping Upland Road, and it was in order to encourage trade that the monks of Waltham Abbey—owners of Epping—developed the modern town of Epping on what was then Epping Heath. In 1253 trade was stimulated by the granting of rights to hold a Friday market, later changed to Monday, and an annual fair. The fairs continued in some shape or form into the early 20th century, but the market is still going strong, though cattle were last sold in 1961.

The Epping market may well have been set up to rival the market at Ongar, first heard of in 1287, but probably older. The de Lucy family inherited Ongar and vigorously built up their estate, extending the castle defences to encompass the whole town, and developing a deer park to the west of the town. Ongar was densely populated in 1377, the date of the first poll tax, when 108 taxpayers and their families were crowded inside the town ramparts. Perhaps surprisingly, surrounding villages were even more populous; Stanford Rivers had 180 taxpayers, Navestock 163, Fyfield 143, and there were 134 at Theydon Garnon. The subsequent poll tax assessment for 1381 led of course to the Peasants Revolt, which began in south Essex.

Small medieval markets were also held at Theydon Garnon and Theydon Mount. Monastic enterprise was dominated by the nearby Abbey of Waltham Holy Cross, but there was another Augustinian priory within our area, at Blackmore, founded in the late 12th century, and dedicated to St Laurence. By the time of its dissolution in 1525 it was only a small establishment, with one prior and three canons. The dissolution of Waltham Abbey in 1540 meant considerable changes in land ownership across the area. Epping and Copped Hall manors passed to the Heneage family.

During the Civil War, Epping was a focus for High Church Anglicanism, which ran against the popular mood of Puritanism in Essex; Epping's High Church vicar, Thomas Holbeach, was thrown out in 1642. There was a minor skirmish at Epping in 1648, where Royalists trying to join up with Lucas and Lisle's ill-fated expedition to Colchester was attacked by Epping Parliamentarians. The Royalists had the best of it, and there were no casualties.

The area was quietly prosperous during the Agrarian Revolution, and numerous large country houses flourished. Ongar expanded, and the improvement of the main road through Epping created more coach traffic which brought prosperity to the town.

In the mid-Victorian period, Epping had the worst death rate from infectious diseases in Essex and there was a long struggle to improve social conditions. Philanthropic landowners such as the Archer-Houblons built village schools and other facilities, but it was left to Epping's local doctor, Joseph Clegg, to wage a long campaign for clean water supplies and proper drainage. Modern hospital facilities had to wait until the 20th century, and even then it is noteworthy that St Margaret's Hospital was formerly the Epping Union workhouse.

The arrival of the railway in 1865 revived a town that was felt by contemporaries to be in decline and a further boost to the town's fortunes was the opening of Epping Forest to the public from 1878. Epping is not in fact the main gateway to the Forest, but that hardly deterred the hordes of trippers who picnicked on Bell Common or The Green at Theydon Bois as they explored the further reaches of London's suburban railway system.

The closing years of the 19th century saw the setting up of modern local government for the area. Epping Rural District Council was born in 1894, as was Ongar Rural District Council. Epping Town got its own Urban District Council two years later, and in 1955 the two rural districts were amalgamated to form Epping and Ongar Rural District. It is the boundaries of that body which form the setting for this particular volume. Following local government changes in 1974, a new local authority was created, Epping Forest District Council, which covered substantially the same area as the old Epping & Ongar district with the addition of Chigwell, Loughton and Buckhurst Hill.

This century has been one of staggering change for the area, and here the pictures speak for themselves. Much that was loved by generations has been swept away, but the quintessential landscape remains, set with towns and villages in which delights of our Essex heritage still cluster thickly. The area has been praised by George Borrow, Arthur Morrison, William Morris, Edward North Buxton, and many other writers, but it is perhaps best to leave the last word to poor, sad, inspired John Clare:

I love the Forest and its airy bounds,
Where friendly Campbell takes hi daily rounds ...
... I love to see the Beech Hill mounting high,
The brook without a bridge, and nearly dry.
There's Buckhurst Hill, a place of furze and clouds
Which evening in a golden blaze enshrouds.

I loved the forest walks and beechen woods,
Where pleasant Stockdale showed me far away
Wild Enfield Chase and pleasant Edmonton.
While giant London, known to all the world,
was nothing but a guess among the trees,
Though only half a day from where we stood.
Such is ambition! Only great at home
And hardly known to quiet and repose.

# *Early History*

Ambresbury Banks lies in the heart of Epping Forest, a hilltop monument to the lost politics of Iron-Age Britain. Although today it sits in dense vegetation, this massive fortification must at that time have had a clear view of the surrounding countryside, implying that heavy pollarding was practised even then. The camp was re-fortified in the turbulent post-Roman years, and it has been suggested that the name derives from Ambrosius Aurelianus, a British warlord who rallied forces against the Saxons in the mid-fifth century. There is a string of defensive points across Essex (and Sussex and elsewhere) with place-names stemming from a root *Ambros-*, so it may be that this place was a staging post in the desperate struggle against Germanic invaders.

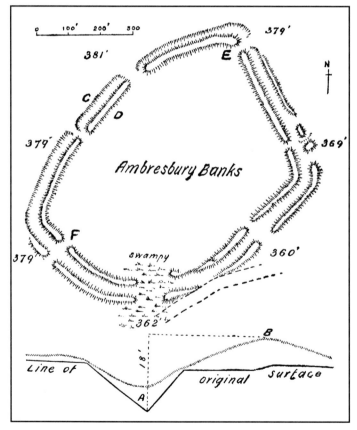

Something of the religion of those—ultimately successful—invaders can be seen in our area, in the pagan stone at Beauchamp Roding. The lack of natural stone in the area made glacial erratics like this boulder all the more noticeable. Many became objects of veneration; St Augustine mentions the fact that the Anglo-Saxons revered standing stones, and it is well known that they were worshipped in the prehistoric period. There is further evidence of pagan belief in the name Nickerlands, in Stanford Rivers, which derives from *nicor*, the Anglo-Saxon word for a water-sprite.

**1** Ambresbury Banks. This plan was made after General Pitt-Rivers' excavation of the fortification in 1881. The 12-acre site has been excavated several times since, and these digs have shown that the south-west entrance (marked 'F' on this plan) is the original Iron-Age gateway. There was also a natural spring within the site.

**2** Ambresbury Banks. The distance between the top of the ramparts and the bottom of the ditch was once 5.5 metres (18 feet), and, though rather less now, is still impressive. Local legend persists that rebel British Queen Boudica ('Boadicea') met her end here after an epic battle with Roman legionaries.

**3** Ambresbury Banks. The formidable Iron-Age ramparts have been transformed into a pleasant woodland prospect for an Edwardian lady and her baby in this 1908 postcard.

**4** Pagan stone in Beauchamp Roding churchyard. The author stands beside a boulder deposited during the Ice Age. The stone is on a prominent hilltop site and, according to local folklore, attempts to move it down to the bottom of the hill met with failure. As the church stands right beside the stone, this tale may reflect garbled memories of a conflict between paganism and Christianity in The Rodings.

**5** Greensted Church. For some years, this lovely church has been held up as the only example of a surviving Saxon timber church. Unfortunately a thorough analysis of the timber has shown that the building in fact dates to just after the Norman Conquest. However, with its stave-built walls, it remains a unique example of this particular architectural style in Britain, and pre-dates by some centuries similar examples in Scandinavia. The puzzle now is why the church was built in what must have been an archaic style.

.VIII. ꝶ **TERRÆ** Canonicoꝝ sčē Crucis de Waltham　　Hundret de
Walthā . Epingam . ten& sēp . sča crux . ꝑ . m̄ . 7 . II . hid . 7 . xv . ac̓ ; Sēp
. I . car̓ 7 . dim̄ in dn̄io . 7 . II . bor . 7 . II . ſer . Silu . L . por . III . ac̓ . p̄ti . x . an.

**TERRA** . Roḃtı filij Corbutionis . Hund̄ de ḃdeſtapla . **Doddenhenc**
ten& Girard̄ de . R . qđ tenuit Aluric libe̓ . t̓ . r̓ . e̓ . ꝑ man̓ . 7 . ꝑ . I . hid̄ . 7 . xvII . ac̓ .
Sēp . I . car̓ . Silu̓ . xx . por . Vaɫ . xx . ſoɫ.

ꝶ Hund̄ de Hangra . Senleiam ten& Rainald̄ . de Goisfrido qđ
tenuit Leuedai . ꝑ . Man̄ . 7 . ꝑ LxxX . ac̓ . 7 . n̄ fuit de feudo an̄gari . ſ; tantū
fuit hō ſuus . Tč . IIII . uiɫt . m̄ . v . m̄ . v . bord . Tč . II . ſer . m̄ . III . Tč . 7 ꝑ̓ .
. II . car̓ . in dn̄io . m̄ . I . Tč . in̄t hōes . I . car̓ . m̄ . II . Silu . cL . porc̓ . xx . ac̓ . p̄ti̓ .
Tč 7 ꝑ̄ uaɫ . Lx . ſoɫ . m̄ . IIII . liḃ.

**6** *Top*. Domesday entry for Epping. The manor of Epping was owned by the monks of Waltham Abbey. Translated, the text reads: 'Hundred of WALTHAM. Holy Cross has always held EPPING as a manor; 2 hides (an area of measurement) and 15 acres. Always 1½ ploughs in lordship; 2 smallholders; 2 slaves. Woodland, 50 pigs; meadow, 3 acres. 10 cattle, 1 cob, 20 pigs, 20 sheep, 8 goats. Value 15s.'

**7** *Middle*. Domesday entry for Doddinghurst. Robert son of Corbucion owned this manor, which the Normans called 'Doddinghene'. Translated, the text reads: 'Hundred of BARSTABLE. Gerard holds Doddinghurst from Robert, which Aelfric held freely before 1066 as a manor, for 1 hide and 17 acres. Always 1 plough. Woodland, 20 pigs. Value, 20s.'

**8** *Bottom*. Domesday entry for Shelley. Shelley formed part of Geoffrey de Mandeville's extensive Essex domain. The text reads: 'Hundred of ONGAR. Reginald holds SHELLEY from Geoffrey, which Leofday held as a manor, for 80 acres. It was not (part) of Asgar's Holding; he was only his man. Then 4 villagers, now 5; now 5 smallholders; Then 2 slaves, now 3. Then and later 2 ploughs in lordship, now 1. Then among the men 1 plough, now 2. Woodland, 150 pigs; meadow, 20 acres. Value then and later 60s; now £4.

**9** Domesday entry for Ongar. Count Eustace of Boulogne owned the manor of Ongar in 1086, and it was clearly a place of some substance. The translation of the text reads: 'Hundred of ONGAR. Aethelgyth held (Chipping) Ongar for 1 hide, as one manor. Now the Count (holds it) in lordship. Always 8 villagers, 8 smallholders, 3 slaves; 2 ploughs in lordship; 3 men's ploughs. Woodland, 1000 pigs; meadow, 28 acres. 2 cobs, 10 cattle, 36 pigs, 112 sheep. Value then 100s; now £8. In the same (Ongar) 1 free man held ½ hide which was this manor's. Now Ralph Baynard holds it.' Further entries relate to Laver ('Laghefara'), Lambourne ('Lamburna'), and Fyfield ('Fifhida').

ꝶ Angrā tenuit Ailida . ꝑ . I . hid̄ . 7 . ꝑ uno Man . M comeſ ia dn̄io . Sēp
vIII . uiɫt . 7 . vIII . bor 7 . III . ſer . 7 . I: . car̄ in dn̄io . 7 . III . car̓ hominum
Silu . ꝏ . porc̓ . xxvIII . ac̓ . p̄ti . II . runc̄ . x . an̄ . xxxvI . porc̓ . cxII . oü.
Tč uaɫ . c . ſoɫ . m̄ . vIII . liḃ.
In Ead . tenuit . I . liḃ hō . dim̄ . hid̄ . que fuit de hoc manerio . m̄ ten&
Rad̄ baignard̄.
ꝶ Laghefarā ten& Ricard̄ de comite qđ tenuit briċtmar ꝑ . xL.
ac̓ . 7 . ꝑ uno Maner̓ . Sēp . I . ſer̓ . 7 . I . car̓ . vI . ac̓ . p̄ti . Vaɫ . x . ſoɫ.
ꝶ Lamburnā ten& Dauid de Comite qđ tenuit Lefsi̓ . ꝑ uno Man̄ .
7 . ꝑ . II hid̄ . 7 . LxxX . ac̓ . Sēp . I . uiɫt . Tč . x . bor . m̄ . xII . Sēp . I . ſer̓ . 7 . II .
car̓ . in dn̄io . 7 . I . car̓ . hom̄ . Silu . c . porc̓ . xx . ac̓ . p̄ti . Tč uaɫ xL . ſoɫ . m̄ . Lx̓.
In dn̄io . Ix . an̄ . 7 . LxxX . oü.
ꝶ Fifhidā . ten& Ricard̄ . de comite qđ tenuit Briċtmar̓ . ꝑ . xL . ac̓ . t̓ . r̓ . e̓ .
7 . ꝑ uno maner̓ . Sēp . III . ſer̓ . 7 . I . car̓ . in dn̄io . Silu . xxIIII . porc̓ . xx . ac̓
p̄ti . Tč̓ . uaɫ . x . ſoɫ . m̄ . xx . Qđā liḃ ten . x . ac̓ . ſ; Ing̓ . iuaſit . sēp . III . ſer . filu . xxIIII . por
ꝶ Fifhidā ten& Junan de comite qđ tenuit Aluuin . t̓ . r̓ . e̓ . ꝑ . uno . ꝏ̄ .
7 . ꝑ . LxxX . ac̓ . Sēp . I . uiɫt . Tč . IIII . bor . m̄ . vI . Sēp . II . ſer . 7 . I . car̓ . in dn̄io .
7 . I . car̓ . hom̄ . Silu . L . porc̓ . x . ac̓ . p̄ti . Tč uaɫ . xxx . ſoɫ . m̄ . xL.

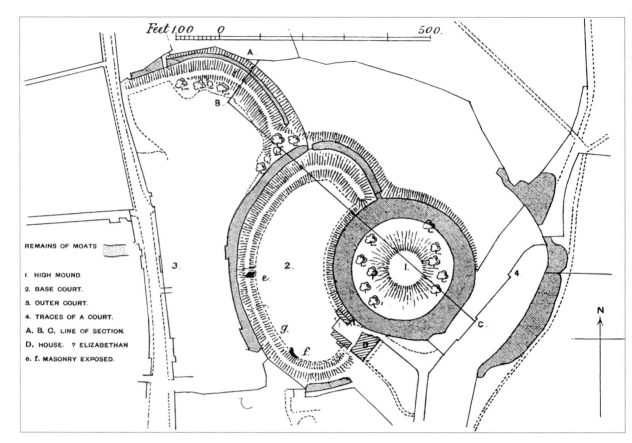

Feet 100 0 500.

REMAINS OF MOATS

1. HIGH MOUND
2. BASE COURT.
3. OUTER COURT.
4. TRACES OF A COURT.
A. B. C. LINE OF SECTION.
D. HOUSE. ? ELIZABETHAN
e. f. MASONRY EXPOSED.

N

10 Ongar Castle. The central mound was occupied by Count Eustace's citadel after the Norman Conquest, but it was the de Lucy family which extended the earthworks out around the town. This was a symbol of Ongar's high status rather than a strictly defensive measure.

11 Ongar Castle mound. Little now remains of the Castle's original grandeur, apart from the steep slopes of the motte and the surrounding moat.

**12** 'Druid Temple' on Navestock Heath. William Stukeley (1687-1765) is thought of as the father of archaeology, and he investigated many important prehistoric and Roman sites across Britain. Unfortunately in later life he became obsessed with 'Druids'. At Navestock Common he thought he had discovered a Druid 'Alate Temple' (i.e. circular temple with wing-shaped projections). There is no trace of such a structure now and it is not clear what, if anything, Dr. Stukeley found, though it was certainly not a Druid temple!

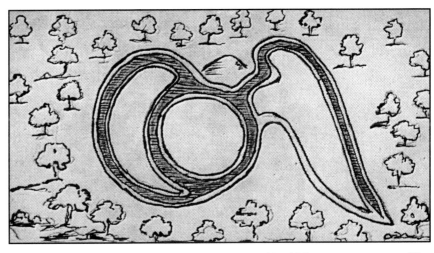

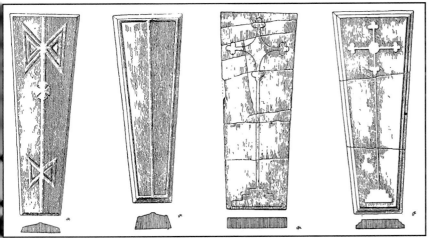

**13** 13th-century stone coffin-slabs. These are unusual in Essex, given the lack of local stone, and they indicated the burial of someone of high rank. The two on the far left come from Stapleford Tawney and Willingale Spain. The nearest two are both from Navestock.

**14** Epping in 1669. This view shows the town seen from what is now Palmers Hill. The scene is much as Pepys saw it when he stayed in Epping in 1659. Plague struck the town in 1665, with many deaths resulting.

# Churches

The sheer variety of parish churches in the area covered by this book is one of its most delightful aspects. A tour of our churches—from the humble rusticity of Greensted's timber staves, to the stately pomp of St John's Church, Epping—is virtually a tour of architectural history.

The area's ecclesiological heritage is rich, particularly from the Norman period. Blackmore's striking timber tower is unique, but the church originated as an Augustinian Priory in the 12th century. The flint walls with herringbone brick coursing at Stondon Massey betray their origins c.1100. Lambourne's half-hidden church is an architectural gem according to no less an authority than Nikolaus Pevsner; here there is a fine Norman door. There is another delightfully ornate Norman door at High Ongar.

Theydon Mount is notable for its monument to the Smyth family, while neighbouring Theydon Garnon boasts an exceptional early memorial brass (William Kirkeby, d. 1458). Theydon Bois has a rare example of a Royal coat-of-arms pre-dating the Commonwealth. The churches at Willingale Spain and Willingale Doe present a unique appearance as they stand side by side (though *not* in the same churchyard as so often claimed). There are various delightful legends about why two churches should be built next to each other (including a tale about two sisters who quarrelled and each built her own church!), but it remains unclear just why they are so close.

The timber church of St Andrew, Greensted, has an astonishing story. It was long thought to be the only surviving example of a timber Saxon church in the country. Historians connected the building of the church with the martyrdom of St Edmund in 870 or, at latest, with the return of St Edmund's body from London to East Anglia in 1013 (the body had been kept in London during the 'Danelaw'). Apparent proof was furnished by an American investigator who provided a date of 845 for the felling of the timbers. However, a recent thorough scientific analysis of the tree-rings in the timbers showed that they *post-date* the Norman Conquest by a few years. A number of mysteries now present themselves. The American archaeologist cannot now be traced, and it is not clear why such a Saxon style of architecture was built under Norman rule, or whether there is still any relationship to St Edmund. Is the little church a copy of an earlier shrine to St Edmund on the site, or perhaps the new Norman landlord could only afford local carpenters for his manorial chapel in this remote spot?

Let us not forget the churches of Epping and Ongar. In Epping the nonconformist tradition is strong, and there are numerous chapels of interest along the High Street, including the Quaker meeting house in Hemnall Street built in 1845. Nonconformity was a powerful force in Ongar too—an Ongar man, one Ralph Jackson, was burnt at the stake in 1556—but it is the Congregationalist link which is best known, thanks to the Taylor family and the studentship of David Livingstone. The parish church of St Martin contains some hidden delights, however, such as the tomb of Italian diplomat Horatio Pallavicino, whose son Tobias also lies there with his wife Jane Cromwell, cousin of the Protector.

**15** Epping Upland Church, *c.*1903. Dedicated to All Saints, this was Epping's original mother church. The present building dates from the 13th century, though it was heavily restored in 1878.

**16** Epping Upland Church. The ivy has been removed in this later view, which dates from about the time that Epping Upland became a separate parish in 1912.

**7** *Left.* The Chapel of St John's, Epping. Epping Town had possessed its own chapel-of-ease since the 14th century, enlarged several times before finally being rebuilt in an ornate castellated fashion in 1832.

**8** *Below.* St John's Church, Epping. St John's became the parish church in 1889 (until then, All Saints Epping Upland formally remained the parish church), and the present edifice was built on a different alignment to the earlier chapel. The tower was added in 1909.

**19** High Beach Church. Strictly speaking part of Waltham Holy Cross rather than Epping, nevertheless this church lies deep in the heart of Epping Forest. First built in 1836 near the present site but at the foot of the hill, the church, dedicated to St Paul, suffered from damp and had to be rebuilt on its present location in 1873, with a new dedication to the Holy Innocents. The church was excluded from those clauses in the Epping Forest Act of 1878 which meant that all land taken from the forest for building had to be returned to the forest.

**20** Ongar Church. In this unusual postcard view, the church spire peeps out from behind the medieval buildings of Ongar High Street. The church, St Martin's, is mainly Norman, though the weatherboarded tower and shingle spire is 15th century. An unfortunate incident occurred at the church *c.*1284. While John the clerk was ringing the church bell, the clapper fell on him and killed him. The value of the bell and clapper was recorded as 8s. 2d.!

**21** Epping Methodist Church. Nonconformity in Epping can trace its history back to at least 1667, when Quakers were holding meetings there. The Methodist link goes back to 1815. An iron church was built in 1878, to be replaced by this brick building in the High Street in 1887.

DR. LIVINGSTONE'S ROOM. ONGAR.

CONGREGATIONAL CHURCH

**22** Ongar Congregational Church. Congregationalism was a powerful force in Ongar's history. The original meeting house was built in 1720, but was replaced in 1833; the building lies through this picturesque archway at the rear of these cottages. The plaque above the arch notes a link with David Livingstone, who trained as a missionary there in 1838-39. Later famed as a fearless explorer, he was more diffident in those early days; sent to preach at Stanford Rivers Congregational Chapel in 1839, he could only stammer, 'Friends, I have forgotten what I have to say' before fleeing.

**23** Epping Roman Catholic Church. This church, dedicated to The Immaculate Conception, is a modern one completed in 1954.

**24** Theydon Bois Church. The original parish church stood next to Theydon Hall and, though later known as St Mary's, may originally have been dedicated to St Botolph. It was largely a 12th-century structure. A more convenient church was built in 1843, but had to be demolished because of poor workmanship in 1850, to be replaced with the present building in 1851, designed by Sidney Smirke. This engraving, of the first church, was made for Elizabeth Ogborne's *History of Essex*, published in 1814.

**25** Blackmore Church. Dedicated to St Lawrence, Blackmore Church is world-famous for its pagoda-like timber tower. The tower was built in the 15th century, and added to the Norman nave which is all of significance that is left of Blackmore Priory. It was to Blackmore that Henry VIII was said to have come in pursuit of Elizabeth Blount, lady-in-waiting to Catherine of Aragon. Henry Fitzroy, their son, was born at the Priory.

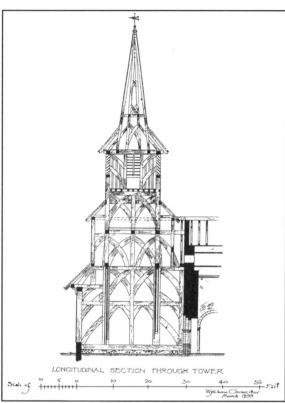

LONGITUDINAL SECTION THROUGH TOWER

Scale of [10 5 0 10 20 30 40 50 feet]

Wykeham Chancellor
March 1899

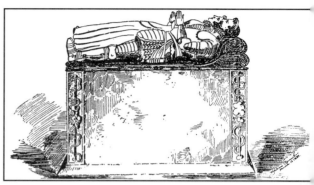

**26** *Left*. Tower of Blackmore Church. This section shows the elaborate medieval timber-work which supports the tower. Ten massive posts hold up the structure, with arched braces acting as cross-beams.

**27** *Above*. The Smyth tomb, Blackmore Church. This fine altar tomb of alabaster commemorates Thomas Smyth and his second wife Margaret. Thomas was son of John Smyth who was granted Blackmore Priory in 1540, following its dissolution in 1525.

**28** *Below*. Bobbingworth Church. Bobbingworth is pronounced Bovinger and, hedging their bets, local road-signs in the area use both spellings. The church of St Germain, in rather striking different shades of brick, dates mainly from the 17th century, though re-faced in the 19th century. The tower was added in 1841.

**29** Coopersale Church. This little church, dedicated to St Alban, was built through the generosity of the Archer-Houblon family who lived nearby in Coopersale House. It was built and consecrated in 1852.

S.W. ANGLE OF NAVE

ELEVATION NORTH SIDE OF CHURCH.    SCALE 4 FT.

**30** *Above left.* Fyfield Church. This unusual looking church sits across the road from the 13th-century Hall, with arcades of the same century though the nave is earlier. The considerable bulk of the church is a reminder of the importance of Fyfield in the middle ages, when it was one of the most populous villages in the hundred.

**31** *Left.* Greensted Church. This postcard view of the south side dates from about 1902. By tradition, the church was built as a resting-place for the body of St Edmund when it was moved from London to Bury St Edmunds in 1013, but tree-ring analysis of the timbers has shown that it must have been built shortly *after* the Norman Conquest. The brick chancel is 12th-century, the wooden tower 15th- or 16th-century. The dormer windows were added in 1848.

**32** *Above.* Greensted Church. In this 19th-century view of the north side, the split-log staves can be clearly seen. Even though it has now been re-dated to the late 11th century, this church remains the oldest timber church in Europe.

**33** *Right.* Timber walls of Greensted Church. This drawing made in 1748 shows the original west wall of the church, now preserved inside the building by the later addition of the tower.

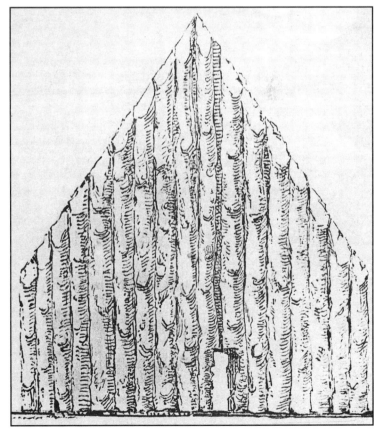

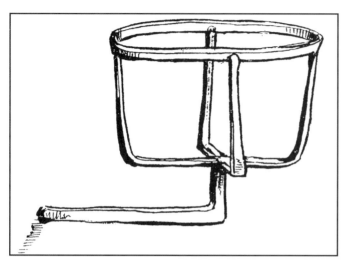

**34** Hourglass stand from Norton Mandeville Church. Once a common feature in churches, these iron hourglass stands are now increasingly rare. They were usually placed in a prominent location close to the pulpit, and the hour of sand often proved too short for sermons of the 17th and 18th centuries!

**35** Stondon Massey Church. Stondon means 'stone-hill', and the village is surnamed Massey after the de Marci family, local Norman landowners. The parish is a small one, made famous by its connection with composer William Byrd (1543-1623). The church is Norman, with the addition of a dainty weatherboarded belfry in the 15th century.

# The Forest

The 6,000 acres which comprise Epping Forest dominate the eastern part of our area, and indeed, the forest has taken its name from the town of Epping since the 17th century. Before that it was Waltham Forest, and earlier still, the Forest of Essex. The royal hunting grounds called Forests were created by the Norman kings; nowadays the word 'forest' is used as a synonym for woodland, but in medieval eyes it meant any land covered by the complex system of Forest laws which gave the monarch the right to hunt deer there. Hence the 'Forest of Essex' was not literally a belt of trees stretching between London and Colchester, and the actual wooded extent of Epping Forest has probably varied very little since Norman times.

Contrary to popular belief, the king never *owned* the Forests, and the local landowner or commoners always retained the rights to exploit the land and the timber. Fallow deer were specifically introduced to Britain by the Normans for hunting purposes, and of course can still be found in Epping Forest. There were red deer too until the early 19th century. Besides the deer, the Forest's primary resource was its wood and timber. Samuel Pepys, as an official of the Navy Board, was brought to see the Forest in 1662, and saw for himself how timber could be cut and sold short, much to his horror. The oak, beech and hornbeam woodland was a carefully husbanded resource, managed by cyclical coppicing and pollarding.

Close to Epping Forest lie the fragments of Ongar Great Park. Like 'forest', the word 'park' was given a very specific meaning in medieval law; these were privately owned areas of land set aside specially for keeping deer, and surrounded by deep ditches to confine the deer. Ongar Great Park originated in Saxon times and was built up almost as a personal fiefdom in the high middle ages by the de Rivers family. Sadly the Park was virtually destroyed in about 1950.

As the centuries passed, the monarchy had less and less interest in hunting, and the royal hunting rights were sold to local landowners. The picturesque Forest courts fell into a decline, and Forest officials with Ruritanian-sounding titles were either not appointed or regarded their jobs as sinecures. By the 19th century, emboldened by the neglect, landowners were inclosing Forest land and turning it over to cultivation or building. However, this was precisely at the time when the Romantic Movement was re-discovering nature and wild places, and an outcry went up about the destruction of the Forests. From humble local residents, too, there was trouble. Inclosure denied them their ancient right to lop timber for building and firewood, and villagers in nearby Loughton went to prison in the 1860s in pursuit of these ancient rights.

Eventually the Corporation of London lent its weight to the struggle to preserve the Forest, and their action resulted in the passing of the Epping Forest Act in 1878, which gave the Corporation control of the Forest, with a duty to conserve its natural aspect and retain it as an open space for public enjoyment. In 1882 Queen Victoria herself visited the Forest to dedicate it to the public for ever.

**36** A stand of pollarded trees. Before it was opened to the public in 1882, Epping Forest's timber resource was managed through pollarding and coppicing. Since then, however, there has been little of this type of woodland maintenance, and many pollards have become top-heavy.

**37** Birch and bracken. The 'natural' trees of Epping Forest are oak, beech and hornbeam, but some areas which were formerly open, cattle-grazed heath have been invaded by birch and bracken. Cattle-grazing has recently been re-introduced to some parts of the forest on an experimental basis to restore former heath.

**38** Deer in Epping Forest. The forest is host to a vast range of animal species, but the most famous is the unique herd of black fallow deer.

**39** Forest parish cattle marks. Inhabitants of parishes within the ancient bounds of the Forest had the right to graze cattle in the Forest, provided the beasts were branded with a mark identifying the parish. Each parish used a letter of the alphabet surmounted by a crown.

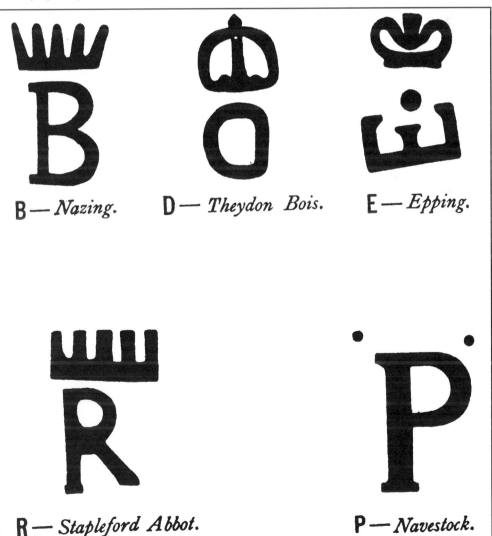

B — *Nazing.*

D — *Theydon Bois.*

E — *Epping.*

R — *Stapleford Abbot.*

P — *Navestock.*

**40** King Harold's Oak and Queen Victoria's Oak. The culmination of Queen Victoria's visit to the forest in 1882 to declare it open to the public was a tree-planting ceremony in High Beach; King Harold's Oak was popularly believed to have been planted by Harold II. Both trees have since died, King Harold's Oak apparently because it was cut up piecemeal to make souvenir snuff boxes! Queen Victoria's Oak was replaced.

**41** Epping New Road. The Epping Highway Trust built this road directly through the heart of the forest in 1830-34, thus avoiding the steep gradients in the Loughton area and opening up a more direct route from London.

**42** Bell Common. This open area to the south west of Epping is a surviving fragment of Epping Heath, and formed part of the preserved Epping Forest in 1878. The survival of even this remnant was threatened by the building of the M25, but the motorway was, after local protests, pushed through via a cut-and-cover tunnel. The cricket pitch on the site was re-instated. The Common takes its name from a hostelry no longer in existence, but there is still a golden bell inn-sign outside the Post House hotel now on the site. In the distance the Epping water tower, built in 1872, can be seen; this is one of the town's most prominent landmarks, now rivalled by the District Council Offices at the other end of the High Street.

**43** Griffin's Wood Cottages. These cottages facing Bell Common were built by the Wythes family, owners of Copped Hall, for workers on their estate. The cottages date from the time when the road to Copped Hall was altered to pass Wood House, built by the Wythes in 1898.

**4** *Left.* Gipsies. In the 19th century the forest was a popular resort for gipsies, who were both feared for their supposedly criminal ways and admired for their romantically close-to-nature lifestyle. Their encampments such as this one often drew tourists.

**5** *Below.* The Pond, Theydon Bois. Theydon Bois lies south of Epping and, although not heavily afforested, is a Forest parish. The pond on the village green was an ideal place for small boys to practise their fishing. Cows are dotted across the green in this Edwardian postcard.

# Industry

A glance at the map shows that the Epping Forest district has a predominantly rural aspect. The Rodings were described as the best plough country in England in the 19th century, so not surprisingly agriculture predominates as the main 'industry' of the area. As the illustrations below show, however, there has always been some industrial activity, particularly around Epping. Even in the Forest itself, there was large-scale sand and gravel extraction until 1878, as well as brickmaking and tile-making and many enterprises connected with timber.

Other industries might be described as 'secondary agricultural businesses', where foodstuffs and other farm products were processed. Brewing was an important local industry; at Marden Ash, Palmers had a brewery at the end of the 19th century, while at Lambourne, Abridge Brewery traced its origins back to 1729. Milling too was a vital link in the processing chain, and many parishes had windmills; there were no less than three at Stanford Rivers, while Stapleford Abbots had two, and Bobbingworth, Epping, Fyfield, Kelvedon Hatch, Moreton, Nazeing, Stapleford Tawney, and Theydon Garnon had one apiece.

**46** *Left*. Cottis Iron Works. Cottis Iron Works was the only real example of heavy industry in Epping. William Cottis established the family firm in 1858 when he built a foundry behind the High Street, and the company grew until it was the largest employer in Epping. Cottis made a vast range of metal products which were exported throughout the world, including not only the agricultural implements described in this 1893 advertisement, but also lawnmowers, coffee processing machines, wrought-iron gates, lamp-posts and railings, and bicycles.

**47** *Above*. Cottis hay sweep. One of Cottis' more unusual products was this hay sweep to be attached to the front of a car.

**48** *Right*. Epping Sanitary Steam Laundry. Until the advent of washing machines, Epping's better-off folk made use of the 'country laundry with a high-class reputation'; this firm was the largest and best-known of several laundries in the town. Laundries were often an important source of work for married women before 1939.

**49**  Matthews' Ongar Mills. Milling was always an important industry in south-west Essex. Here the horse-draw
carts of Matthews' Mills are lined up proudly for the camera in Ongar High Street.

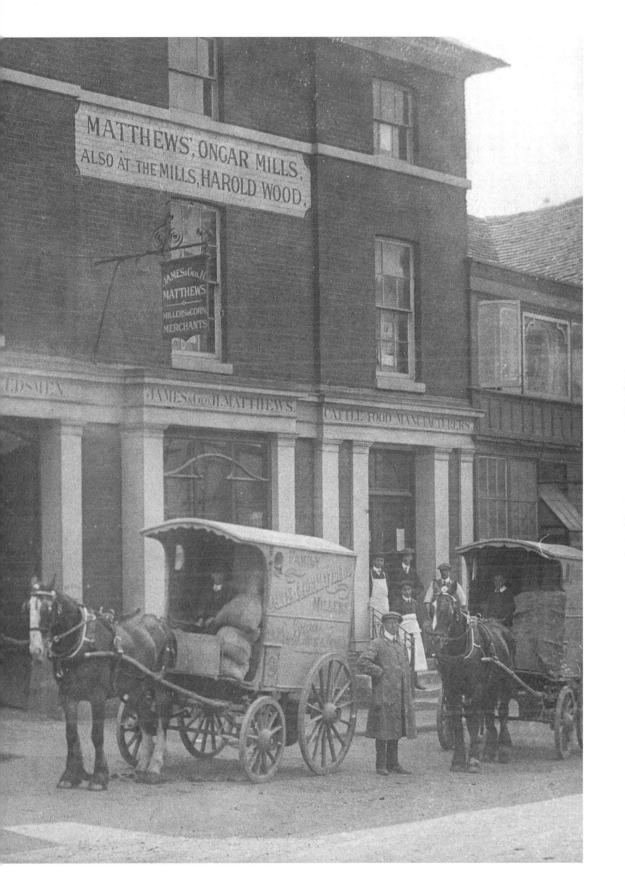

**50** *Left*. Lorry from Matthews' Mills. The company were eager users of steam motor vehicles. But this solid-tyred monster came a cropper when it hit a tree!

**51** *Below left*. Local tradesmen's advertisements. Agricultural services predominated in the rural villages, and an important part of the local watchmaker's trade was the repair of church tower clocks.

**52** *Below*. Epping farmworkers. A rare photograph of agricultural workers celebrating the end of haymaking, *c.*1901. The photograph was taken in the Charles Street area of Epping, then open fields.

**53** Toot Hill Mill. This mill was one of three which once stood in the parish of Stanford Rivers, and dates from 182. A horrific accident at the mill in 1829 attracted nationwide press coverage. The mill was struck by lightning whic caused the stored grain to explode. The miller, one Joseph Knight, was horribly injured, being found with his le hanging off 'connected with his body by a small portion of flesh only', his head 'most shockingly and indescribab lacerated' and his right hand 'mangled in a most frightful manner'. The report continued 'Upon further examinatio large splinters of wood and even grains of wheat were found driven into various parts of his body'. Despite his injurie Knight survived, though he lost a leg. The mill itself was rebuilt and lasted until 1935.

**54** Toot Hill Mill. Another view, looking across fields.

# Inns

The public house has been one of the foci of parish life for centuries, and the pictures below show a cross-section of village inns. Inns had another important function, however, as travellers' rests and, as the last major coaching stop on the road to London, Epping had more taverns than most towns of a similar size. Although the arrival of the railways gave a new lease of life to Epping's inns, the most notable change in Epping's long High Street over the last century has been the loss of most of its many coaching inns and taverns.

In 1897, there were no less than 27 pubs in the High Street: the *Black Boy*, the *Black Dog*, the *Black Lion*, the *Cock*, the *Crown*, the *Duke of Wellington*, the *Duke of York*, the *George & Dragon*, the *Globe*, the *Golden Lion*, the *Green Man*, the *Half Moon*, the *Harp*, the *Harrow*, the *Horse & Groom*, the *King' Arms*, the *King's Head*, the *Little Cock*, the *Rose and Crown*, the *Star*, the *Sun*, the *Thatched House*, two pubs called the *White Hart*, the *White Horse*, the *White Lion*, and the *White Swan*. Less than half a dozen of these survive today. One inn that successfully made the transformation from horse traffic to motor traffic is of course the *Bell*, now a popular motel.

Another creeping change has been the recent trend to re-name historic pubs with some new and usually incongruous name. This has provoked considerable sound and fury but unfortunately little can be done about the loss of these points of reference in the landscape. Happily, the phenomenon is associated with only a few small breweries and pub companies. The rebuilt *Wake Arms* became *City Limits*, but locals happily carry on referring to it, and the roundabout on which it stands, by its proper name!

**55** The *Bell*, Epping. This inn was once such a landmark that it gave its name to Bell Common, replacing the earlier name of Beacon Common. Today the old *Bell* inn is overshadowed by an uncompromisingly modern motel block and roosters no longer strut in front of the building as they did in this 1912 view.

**56** The *Cock*, Epping High Street. The brick frontage of this old inn dates from about 1800, but this brick front was superimposed on an earlier timber-framed structure dating from at least the 16th century. The inn closed down in 1961 and the building has since been converted into shops and offices.

**57** *Turpin's Cave*, Epping Forest. According to dubious local tradition, highwayman Dick Turpin and his accomplice Tom King sheltered in Epping Forest in a small cave to avoid capture. A hollow under this inn was claimed by some as the original site of the cave, and the spot became a popular tourist venue. This view is postmarked 1908. The pub was demolished in 1973 and a private house now stands on the site.

58  The *Robin Hood*, Epping Forest. Built *c*.1865 at a crossroads in the heart of the Forest, it was soon attracting large crowds of trippers, as can be seen from this postcard of *c*.1900.

59  The *Wake Arms*, Epping Forest. Another popular tourist venue, named after a prominent local landowning family. This view dates from about 1955. The building has since been replaced by a new café-bar known as 'City Limits', though the road junction is still called the Wake Arms Roundabout.

**60** The *White Hart*, Abridge. This inn was already in existence in 1723. In the foreground is the bridge over the Roding which gave the village its name; in 1086 it was known as Affebrigge, or Aeffa's Bridge. This narrow bridge is late 18th-century and has a Grade II listing.

**61** The *King's Oak*, High Beach. There was an inn of that name on this site in the 18th century, but this building dates from 1887 on a much larger scale to cope with increasing tourism after the forest was opened. It was on the open ground in front of the inn that Queen Victoria declared Epping Forest open in 1882.

52 The *King's Oak*, High Beach. Another view of the inn, still a very popular spot for forest visitors. The open ground behind the pub was at first a cycle track, and in 1928 it was converted into a speedway track, Britain's first.

53 The *King's Head*, North Weald Bassett. A picturesque view, though in fact the timbers of this ancient inn have only been exposed relatively recently; earlier photographs show it stiffly clad in protecting rendering, as indeed were most Essex timber-framed buildings.

**64** *Below*. The *Merry Fiddlers*, Theydon Garnon. This ancient inn gave its name to Fiddlers Hamlet. The building dates from at least the 17th century and this postcard view from about 1908.

**65** *Right*. The *Talbot*, North Weald Bassett. The men of the village have congregated by the door of this historic inn; an aproned man seems to be pushing a cart out of sight behind the hedge. This view dates from *c*.1905. The *Talbot* is a well-known local landmark and popular restaurant, and has given its name to the road junction, now a busy roundabout.

**66** *Below right*. The *Queen's Head*, Fyfield. This view dates from about 1890.

# Houses

The natural beauty of Epping Forest and the Roding valley has long attracted London's wealthy merchants and the area is sprinkled with fine 'parvenu' mansions as well as older, often moated, manor houses. D.W. Coller, writing about Ongar Hundred in 1861, commented on 'the neatness of the buildings, and the many additional ornaments it receives from the number of noblemen's and gentlemen's seats with which it abounds'.

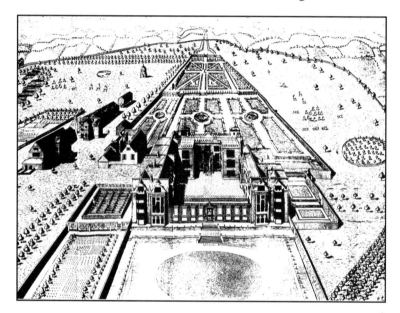

**67** Copped Hall in 1735. The manor of Copped Hall seems to have originated in the mid-12th century, and from 1350 until shortly before the dissolution it was held by the canons of Waltham Abbey. Sir Thomas Heneage, who was granted the manor in 1564, is believed substantially to have rebuilt the Hall; Queen Elizabeth I visited him there in 1568. This engraving shows the appearance of Heneage's hall in its grand emparkment.

The two largest and most outstanding buildings of the area are Copped Hall and Hill Hall, both close to Epping and both, sadly, now derelict shells. Both are landmarks visible from the M25; indeed Copped Hall stands on a singular eminence which must surely call into question the conventional explanation of the name's origin. In his *Place-Names of Essex*, P.H. Reaney claimed that the name originated from *cop* meaning a tower or pinnacle; the historian Fuller noted that the tower had two turrets. However, drawings do not show these turrets as significant architectural features, and the name must surely derive rather from the Anglo-Saxon *copp*, meaning a summit.

On a smaller scale, this part of the county is well stocked with characteristic timber-framed houses. The lack of natural stone in the county and the abundance of woodland meant that here as in almost no other part of England, the carpenter was king in manorial as well as in vernacular architecture. A great many of these houses survive, often as farmhouses, and often moated, a medieval display rather than a defensive feature.

**68**    Copped Hall, *c*.1909. Copped Hall was sold to Edward Conyers in 1739, and subsequently rebuilt about 250 metres from the Heneage building 1748-*c*.1760 by John Conyers I. The Conyers hall was an English country mansion in the grandest manner. This view shows the west front from the Great Causeway, one of the most notable features of the gardens.

**69**    Copped Hall, *c*.1909. This view shows one of the summerhouses, with the ballroom behind. Copped Hall was sold to the Wythes family in 1867, and the house was considerably extended by Edward James Wythes in 1895. In 1917 the house was gutted by fire, and remains a shell to this day, a prominent landmark for passing traffic on the M25. There are, at the time of writing, ambitious plans for its restoration.

**70** Interior of Copped Hall. A corner of the astonishingly ornate conservatory.

**71** Gardens of Copped Hall. This view looks west from the terrace of the west front into the formal gardens. The octagonal basin, one of two, has a fine cedar tree at its centre.

**72** Hill Hall stands in the parish of Theydon Mount, and is indeed on a prominent hill with a commanding view of surrounding countryside. The present house was built by Sir Thomas Smyth (1513-1577), in a grand classical style. Much of the external decoration comprises plaster got up to look like marble and other stonework. Smyth was a fascinating character, one time ambassador to Paris and a confidante of Elizabeth I, though he was later broken, like many a politician before and after him, by attempts to resolve conflicts in Ulster.

**73** Hill Hall. After a period of neglect in the early 20th century—the house was at one time let to the self-styled 'Duke of Moro'—Hill Hall came up for sale in 1924; this extract from the sale catalogue lists some of its many features. During the Second World War, the house was used as a transit camp, then as a prisoner-of-war camp, and it was subsequently turned into a women's prison. Christine Keeler, star of the Profumo Affair in the 1960s, was at one time incarcerated there. The house burnt down on 18 April 1969 and is now a derelict shell.

## 45 MINUTES' MOTOR DRIVE FROM LONDON
### HIGH UP WITH CHARMING VIEWS.

ONE OF THE MOST BEAUTIFUL ELIZABETHAN MANSIONS

within this distance of London.,

## TO BE LET, FURNISHED

with a full complement of servants.

THE HOUSE is one of the best examples of the architecture of the period, is in first-class condition, handsomely appointed, and contains many valuable works of art, including rare furniture, tapestries, pictures, etc.

| | |
|---|---|
| *Great hall,* | *Twelve to fifteen best bedrooms.* |
| *Dining room,* | *Dressing rooms,* |
| *Music room,* | *Ample servants' bedrooms,* |
| *Library,* | *Eight bathrooms,* |
| *Study,* | *Stabling, garage,* |
| *Boudoir,* | *Groom's and chauffeur's quarters,* |

IT IS FITTED WITH MODERN CONVENIENCES, INCLUDING ELECTRIC LIGHT AND EIGHT BATHROOMS,

and garden produce and dairy produce will be supplied at market prices.

### EXQUISITE OLD WORLD PLEASURE GROUNDS,
ADJOINING WHICH IS THE BEAUTIFULLY TIMBERED PARK.

TWO HARD TENNIS COURTS, SQUASH RACQUET COURT, TWO GOLF LINKS IN THE NEIGHBOURHOOD.

All details and terms can be had on application to the Agents, Messrs. WINKWORTH & Co., 48, Curzon Street, Mayfair, London, W. 1.

**74** 'A Little Bit of Old Ongar'. There are many architectural gems in Ongar's town centre, but it is this timber-framed corner building, dated to 1642, which most commonly appears in postcard views. This card was posted in 1915 in nearby Willingale. The message reads: 'We are having a lovely holiday, the weather is perfect + the country looks A-1. The harvesting is in full swing ... fancy Stratford + the City after this!'.

**75** Shelley House. Perhaps inevitably, a petrol station now dominates The Four Wantz, the busy ancient junction north of Chipping Ongar. Not so long ago, however, Shelley House was one of the few buildings in the area. The house stands in the parish of Shelley, and was originally built in the 17th century, the handsome Georgian façade being added in about 1800.

**76** Castle House, Ongar, and The White House were at various times the principal residences of the lords of the manor of Ongar. Castle House was built in the 16th century and is best known as the residence in the 18th and 19th centuries of the 'Taylors of Ongar', a distinguished family of Congregationalists. Isaac Taylor (b.1730) was a skilled engraver, and his second son, also Isaac (1759-1829) followed him into this profession. The wife of Isaac II, Ann Taylor née Martin, was from Shenfield; she wrote several 'good housekeeping' books. Isaac II became a Congregational minister, and moved to Colchester in 1796, then to Ongar in 1811. He too began writing books, works for children, travelogues and biographical works. Jane and Ann followed their parents' literary bent, and wrote the best-selling nursery books *Original Poems for Infant Minds* (1805) and *Rhymes for the Nursery* (1806). Jane's most famous rhyme was *Twinkle, Twinkle Little Star*. Their younger brother Isaac (1787-1865) was well-known as an artist, writer and theologian. Jane never wed, but Anne married the Rev. Joseph Gilbert and moved to Nottingham.

**77** Marshalls Farm, North Weald Bassett. Lying east of Wintry Wood, this timber-framed building was built in the 17th century, though in origin it dates back to a manorial holding of Ralph le Mareschal in the 13th century. The moat seen in the foreground of this view surrounds not the present farm but the site of the earlier building.

**78** *Above*. Vernacular architecture, Matching Green. Matching is a typically well-scattered Essex village, best known for its 15th-century Marriage Feast Room. The whole parish is liberally studded with fine houses, notably around Matching Green, the largest of Matching's several 'ends'. This turn-of-the-century postcard shows a range of interesting buildings ranging from the humble row of medieval timber cottages on the left (later the site of the village post office), to the handsome 18th-century brick house 'The Limes' on the right.

**79** *Left*. Fairmead Lodge. A royal hunting lodge in Epping Forest at least since the 14th century, Fairmead Lodge was a striking weatherboarded building demolished in 1898. The Lodge had since 1853 been a 'refreshment room' run by the Bartholomew family, catering mainly for school and Sunday School parties.

# *People*

The roll of the famous from Epping, Ongar and district, is a distinguished one, and includes the only Essex-born 'royal', an illegitimate son of Henry VIII, as well as Mary Tudor, who lived at Copped Hall for a time. Henry Doubleday (1808-1875) was a pioneering naturalist who used the Forest as a resource to inform his studies and collection. He was well known in the fields of both entomology and ornithology. Thomas Fowell Buxton (1837-1916), who lived at Warlies near Epping, was another great supporter of the natural aspect of Epping Forest, and was a tireless campaigner for its preservation.

Another Epping worthy was Benjamin Winstone (1820-1907), who attended Isaac Payne's Quaker School in Epping, industrial chemist, eminent historian (VP Brit Arch Assoc.), wrote and privately published numerous works on the local history of Epping area. Artists and writers were, not surprisingly, attracted to the Forest area. Mention has already been made in the Introduction of poet John Clare. Tennyson also spent some time at High Beach. The artist Lucien Pissarro (1863-1944) lived for some time at Epping, while Sydney Carter lived at High Beach.

**80** Henry Fitzroy (1519-1536). Born at Blackmore to Elizabeth Blount, one of Catherine of Aragon's ladies-in-waiting, Henry Fitzroy was the illegitimate son of Henry VIII. When it became clear that Catherine of Aragon would not bear him a male heir, Bluff King Hal showered his son with honours, making him Duke of Richmond and Somerset and, at the age of six, he was appointed the King's Lieutenant north of the Trent, responsible for organising the defence of the Scottish borders! Henry Fitzroy seems to have been a studious young man, cultivated by Wolsey. Henry VIII was said to have considered making Fitzroy King of Ireland in preparation for naming him as heir, but, often a sickly youth, he died at the age of 17 in 1536.

**81** *Right*. Thomas Torrell (d. *c*.1442). This memorial brass in the north wall of the chancel of St Christopher's, Willingale Doe, commemorates Sir Thomas Torrell, Sheriff of Essex and Hertfordshire in 1428, who was the founder of a significant local dynasty prominent in medieval Essex life. There is still a Torrell's Hall in Willingale.

**82** *Far right*. Anne Sackville (d. 1582). Another brass from Willingale Doe; this lady was daughter of Humphrey Torrell, a descendant of Thomas Torrell and, like Thomas, he was also Sheriff of Essex and Hertfordshire (in 1503 and 1509).

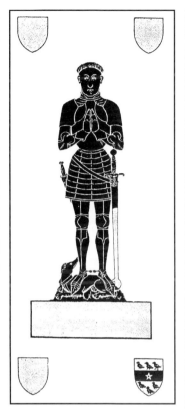

In Ongar, Captain P.J. Budworth, who lived at Greensted Hall, and Henry Gibson J.P., who lived at the White House, were able to exert immense influence over the town's politics during the last century, and it is no exaggeration to say that the present form of the town is partly as a result of their activities. Edward Boodle (1722-1772), founder of the famous London club, is buried in Ongar churchyard. One sporting hero with local connections is William Webb Ellis, who invented the game of rugby; he was rector of Magdalen Laver for 15 years.

The Houblon family had reason to be proud of their ancestor James Houblon, who founded the Bank of England. Industrious Huguenot emigrés, the family prospered and bought up large tracts of west Essex. The family are associated with Moreton, where Jacob Houblon (1634-1698) was rector for 35 years, and Bobbingworth, where another Jacob was also rector a century later. Later the family married into the distinguished Archer family of Coopersale, creating the immensely wealthy Archer-Houblon dynasty.

In recent years, the Epping and Ongar area has again come into vogue as a retreat for the wealthy and famous. Rock star Rod Stewart, computer wizard Alan Sugar, publisher David Sullivan, playwright Ray Cooney, snooker star Steve Davis, and boxer Frank Bruno all live in the area, and there is a veritable constellation of actors and soap stars who have chosen to make their homes in this pleasant part of the world.

**83** *Left*. William Byrd (?1543-1623). This remarkable Tudor composer spent the last 30 years of his life at Stondon Massey, where he lived at Stondon Place. Besides his musical talent, Byrd had a considerable skill for maintaining fairly friendly relationships with the monarchy despite his own Roman Catholicism. In his home village, however, he was not so tactful, being in frequent dispute with his neighbours.

**84** *Below left*. Dick Turpin (1705-1739). Born in Hempstead in north Essex, Dick Turpin led a life of brutal crime. Britain's best known highwayman, much of his 'career' took place in and around Epping Forest. There is no surviving accurate likeness, but this contemporary engraving depicts him hiding in the fabled 'Turpin's Cave', his supposed base deep in the heart of the forest.

**85** *Above*. John Clare (1793-1864). Born in Northamptonshire in extremely humble circumstances, John Clare sprang to overnight renown as a 'peasant poet' taken up by London society from 1820 onwards. Unfortunately his return to obscurity was equally rapid and he suffered mental breakdown. In 1837 he was persuaded to place himself in the hands of Dr. Matthew Allen, then running a private asylum at High Beach on very enlightened lines. His condition improved, and he wrote a stream of pathetically lyrical poetry, but in 1841 he ran away from his carers and walked back to Northamptonshire, where he spent the rest of his life in the county lunatic asylum.

**86** Alfred, Lord Tennyson (1809-1892). Another of the Forest's many literary associations is with Tennyson, who stayed at Beech Hill House, High Beach, from 1837-40. Tennyson worked continuously on his epic masterpiece *In Memoriam* while in High Beach. His famous line 'In the Spring a young man's fancy lightly turns to thoughts of love' is from *Locksley Hall*, written at High Beach, while another ode, *The Talking Oak*, refers more directly to the Forest and its splendid panoramas towards London:

> Beyond the lodge the city lies,
> Beneath its drift of smoke;
> And ah! With what delighted eyes
> I turn to yonder oak.

**87** Epping Forest Keepers, *c*.1878. A splendid body of well-armed men poses shortly after the passage of the Epping Forest Act which opened the forest to the public. From left to right they are: Charles Watkins, J. Chellis (Head Keeper), H. Butt, James Pearce, J. Dunning, Frederick Luffman (Head Keeper) and William D'Oyley (Superintendent).

**88** Forest Gipsies. Reference has already been made to the bands of gipsies which once used to camp in the forest, and here is a splendid photograph of a gipsy family with their ornate *varda* or wagon. Contact between gipsies and cockneys brought Romany words such as tanner ('sixpence') and dooks ('fists' as in 'put up your dooks') into everyday use

**89** Charles Hurford. Epping Forest Urban District Council was established in 1896 covering the civil parish of Epping and part of Epping Upland parish. Dr. Charles Hurford, J.P., was the moving spirit behind these beginnings of modern local democracy and served as the Council's first Chairman. This photograph dates from 1902.

**90** Winston Churchill (1874-1965). Churchill was first elected Member of Parliament for the Epping Division in 1924, and this rare photograph shows him on the hustings on 4 October of that year. He remained Epping's M.P. until 1945 when the constituency was divided and he then sat for the southern division of Woodford. He never lived in the constituency but local esteem for Churchill was so great that he was given the unique honour of a statue within the forest bounds, on Woodford Green.

**91** *Right*. Rod Stewart (b.1945). The jet-setting rock star Rod Stewart has a home on the Copped Hall estate in Epping and is a well-known figure in local public life, turning out for charitable events and supporting various community initiatives.

**92** *Far right*. Alan Sugar (b.1947). A number of well-known public figures have chosen to make their homes in the Epping area, including Alan Sugar, the computer innovator who founded the internationally-renowned electronics corporation Amstrad in 1968.

# Public Services

Until the late 19th century, the church parochial authorities and manorial landlords carried out the business of local administration, which tended to be a haphazard affair, particular where major undertakings such as road maintenance were concerned. The matter which was of most anxiety in the early 19th century was 'The Poor', and Poor Law Unions were set up across the country to administer centralised workhouses. Epping was the centre for one Poor Law Union, and Ongar another.

The story of local government in the town of Epping in particular is inextricably linked with the struggle to provide clean drinking water and to control the frequent epidemics of infectious diseases.

**93** Epping Urban District Council emblem. Epping Urban District Council was formed in 1896, and used this rather striking emblem until its absorption into Epping Forest District Council in 1974.

In 1853, local doctor Joseph Clegg began a 20-year campaign to improve conditions and eradicate the periodic bouts of cholera and typhoid, forcing the building of the landmark water tower and the not-so-visible but equally important wells, sewers and water mains.

Local authorities as we know them today first appeared in 1894, with the creation of Epping Rural District and Ongar Rural District. Two years later, Epping was divided between an Urban and a Rural District Council, with separate offices at either end of the High Street.

**94** Epping Post Office staff, *c.*1907. At that date the post office stood in Station Road in premises which later became the National Westminster Bank. The postmaster, Mr. Sibley, is seated centre, and on his left is Mr. Gallagher, who succeeded him. Mr. E. Cutts sits to his right.

**95** Drinking Fountain, Epping High Street. After a spate of epidemics in late Victorian Epping, efforts were made to improve the area's water supply. This drinking fountain, once a prominent town landmark, was erected to commemorate Queen Victoria's Golden Jubilee in 1887. It was demolished in 1961, ironically as part of a Civic Trust improvement scheme', and now lies buried under a car park.

**96**  The Fountain, Theydon Bois. This splendid drinking fountain, with horse trough close by, was another example of Victorian attempts to provide clean drinking water. The fountain's ornate superstructure was removed in 1906. The whole thing was replaced with a utilitarian concrete structure in the 1930s, and has now disappeared entirely!

# Schools

The provision of education by local authorities began after 1870, but schools in one form or another had existed long before that. There was a striking flowering of educational endeavour as early as the 17th century: two children went up to Cambridge University from Moreton in 1614 as a result of a school there; a school was founded in North Weald Bassett in 1678; in Fyfield, a school for poor children was established in 1692, while in Ongar there was a school as early as 1673, and in 1678 one Joseph King left an endowment to provide for the education of poor boys; the King's Trust School he thus created survived as a thriving independent school until 1913, when it was transferred to the local education authority. In 1798 there was a 'School of Industry' in Epping, though little is known about it, apart from the fact that it was run by a 'Society for Bettering the Conditions and Increasing the Comforts of the Poor'.

Quaker influence was strong in Epping and in the early 19th century there were two Quaker boarding schools in the town. The mid-Victorian period also saw a wave of church provision of schools; Anglican funds set up 'National' schools and nonconformist enterprise created the rival 'British' schools. Like much of Essex, the Epping Forest area was strongly nonconformist though, strangely enough, in Epping itself the National School (which has survived as the St John's Church of England School) was by far the most successful.

In many parts of the area there were little 'dame schools', which provided what little education there was for girls in mid-Victorian Britain. There was for instance a 'School for Ladies' flourishing in Ongar in 1866, while at Theydon Mount the lady of the manor, Mrs. Letitia Bower, personally oversaw the establishment of a school for poor girls in 1826, ten years before a similar venture for local boys!

One of the most interesting educational establishments in the area was at Fyfield. In 1885, here in what was then remote countryside, West Ham Council set up a 'boot camp' school for its toughest truants; as there were few runaways it was deemed a success, and those who underwent the 'short sharp shock' regime at Fyfield still recall the event vividly! In 1925 West Ham converted the school into an open-air school, to which children with rickets and other symptoms of inner-city life were sent to recuperate in the fresh air. Lessons, dinners and even sleeping took place out-of-doors wherever possible.

**97** Isaac Payne's School, Epping. Founded in about 1800, this boarding school for Quakers—one of two in Epping—faced The Green more or less on the site now occupied by the District Council offices. It later lost its Quaker connection, and for a time it was known as Ivy House School, then as Hunter's School, before closing in 1874.

**98** St John's School, Epping. The class of 1902 sit in their starched best, boys with lace collars and girls with smocks under the stern gaze of 'Miss'.

**9** Ongar Grammar School. Situated at the north end of the town on the west side of the High Street, Ongar Grammar School—a public school—was founded in 1811. It was for a time known as Ongar Academy, and under the Clark family, who formed a dynasty of headmasters here for over half a century, grew to considerable status. This advert dates from the turn of the century; 'Diet unlimited' sounds appealing, but the thought of a 'tepid' swimming bath is not so attractive! The baths were added in 1885, and there was a wide range of other facilities, including a rifle range. The school closed in 1940.

## EDUCATION.

# Ongar Grammar School

### TWENTY MILES FROM LONDON.

Pupils receive a thorough Mercantile Education. A Preparatory Class for Little Boys; thirty acres of ground, gravel soil, 200 feet above sea level; pure Milk from own dairy farm. Diet unlimited. Cricket, tennis, fishing.

### SEE PROSPECTUS FOR DETAILS.

### GRAND TEPID SWIMMING BATH.

Terms, 30 Guineas inclusive; Reduction for Brothers.

# Principal - Dr. CLARK.

**100** Theydon Bois School. This establishment originated with a National School built in 1840, which came under the control of Essex County Council in 1902. This delightful class picture dates from 1923.

THEYDON BOIS
SCHOOL
1923

# Shelley House School,

## ONGAR, ESSEX.

Principal - - - - Mrs. MITCHELL.

Mrs. Mitchell is assisted by Certificated English Governesses, a resident French Governess, and Visiting Masters from London.

The system of teaching is based on the newest methods

The Ordinary Course of Study comprises:—

*English Language and Literature, Arithmetic, Mathematics, Geography, Scripture, History, Latin, French, Music, &c.*

### TERMS ON APPLICATION.

Pupils are thoroughly prepared for University Local Examinations, for those held by Trinity College in Practical and Theoretical Music, and for the College of Preceptors.

Ongar, in North Essex, is considered one of the most healthy localities in England. Shelley House is pleasantly situated in six acres of ground, with garden and tennis lawn. A liberal table is provided, and cows are kept for the benefit of the Pupils.

PRIVATE LESSONS BY ARRANGEMENT.

**101** Shelley House School. Note that 'a liberal table is provided' at this school, which began life as a 'ladies academy' founded in about 1860. As the name suggests, tuition was in Shelley House, close to the Four Wantz at Ongar.

**102** The following six photographs show Fyfield Residential Open Air School. Opened in 1885 as a truant school for West Ham, it was converted into an open-air school in 1925. In this view, from c.1936, pupils can be seen at dinner time; note the open sides to the dinner hall.

**103** Pupils enjoying an outdoor art lesson.

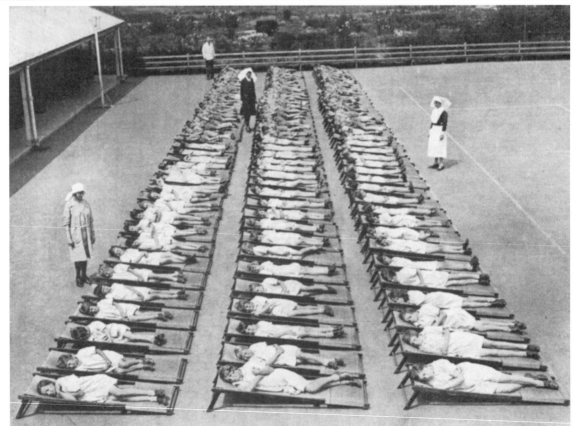

**104** *Above left*. The boys undergo physical jerks ...

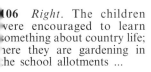

**105** *Below left* ... while the girls enjoy an open-air 'rest period', closely supervised by matron.

**106** *Right*. The children were encouraged to learn something about country life; here they are gardening in the school allotments ...

**107** *Below*. ... and here they are helping with the hay harvest.

**108** Prospect House School. A turn of the century advertisement for another of Epping's many private schools.

**109** Wansfell House. Situated on Piercing Hill in Theydon Bois, Wansfell House is run as an adult education college by Essex County Council.

# Shops, Streets and Views

Views of streets and shops are evergreen provokers of nostalgia, as the changing streetscape is one of the most obvious markers of fluctuating times. Nothing seems to bring back reminiscence and recollection as strongly as vanished shops and shopkeepers past! The passing of stores like Pyne's and Cottis in Epping often seems to mark the end of an era. Change has been a force in the surrounding villages too; like so many other places, they have lost shops and other services, as the photographs below show only too clearly.

The economy of the Epping and Ongar area was of course vitally linked to trade and commerce. The area acted as a sort of filter for raw goods inbound to the capital and for finished goods coming out of London. Epping's market in particular, but earlier the market in Ongar too, were important places for exchange of news as well as merchandise. Even little Theydon Garnon and Theydon Mount once had their own markets.

The sheer range and variety of shops and trades a century ago is startling. The local directory for 1897 listed the following trades in Epping: one aerated water manufacturer, one architect, seven bakers, three blacksmiths, seven bootmakers, one brewer, seven builders, five butchers (including one pork butcher), one carman, three carpenters, four carriage and coach builders, one china warehouseman, four coal merchants, one coffee house manager, one corn merchant, four drapers, six dressmakers, one estate agent/auctioneer, one fishmonger, four 'general dealers', one greengrocer, five grocers, three hairdressers, one hay dealer, one ironmonger, one jobmaster, one milliner, three painters, one plumber, one printer/stationer, 22 publicans, four solicitors, one stonemason, one surveyor, one tailor, one taxidermist, four tobacconist/confectioners, one upholsterer, one watchmaker, one wine and spirit merchant, and one wool stapler.

Ongar boasted a similar range of trades: one auctioneer, three bakers, three black-smiths, five bootmakers, one brewer, one bricklayer, three builders (also listed as undertakers!), three butchers (including one pork butcher), one carpenter, two carriers, one carter, two chemists, one china warehouseman, one chimney sweep, one coachbuilder, two coal merchants, three confectioners, one corn merchant, one cricket outfitter, two drapers, two dressmakers, one florist, one furniture dealer, four grocers, two hairdressers, two harness makers, two ironmongers, one laundry manager, one newsagent/stationer, one nurseryman, one outfitter, three painters, one photographer, one printer/stationer, 10 publicans, one solicitor, two tailors, one tobacconist, one veterinary surgeon, one watchmaker, and one wine merchant.

Even Theydon Bois, a very small village in 1897, boasted a wide spectrum of shops and merchants: one baker, one blacksmith, two builders, one butcher, one carpenter, one draper, one fishmonger, one 'general dealer', one greengrocer, one gro-cer, one house decorator, one laundress, one nurseryman, six publicans, one solicitor, and one wheelwright.

**110** Epping High Street in 1822. This is the earliest-known illustration of St John's as a chapel-of-ease. In the background is the Market House, which was recorded in 1666 and demolished in 1845. There was also a butter cross, demolished in 1781. The *Cock* inn is on the right, with the whipping post in front, while the village stocks stand ominously in the middle of the street.

**111** Epping Market House was one of two wooden market houses which formerly stood in the High Street. This one was pulled down in 1845. A butter cross also once graced the High Street. Epping butter—a by-product of the cattle market—was the town's best known 'export' in the 19th century, and was mentioned approvingly by the poet Thomas Hood.

**112**  Epping Market. The market, first granted in 1253, was predominantly an animal market until the 20th century; not only cattle, but geese and pigs were important to the area's economy. In 1833 there was a case of a wife being sold—for half a crown!—at the market. In this instance, the husband was imprisoned after getting blind drunk on gin from the proceeds, but such affairs were not unknown at other markets in Essex, and were usually a desperate form of pawning by the utterly destitute. The cattle market closed in 1961.

**113**  Epping High Street. This card was posted in 1907, before the tower of St John's was built. Epping Methodist Church can be seen on the left.

**114** Church's butchers. Epping's most famous product is undoubtedly its sausages, long rumoured to be spiced up with a little venison. Church's butchers in Epping High Street have carried on the centuries-old tradition of sausage manufacture and are still thriving to this day. The company was founded in 1888 by Stephen John Church.

**115** Mallinson's clothier's stood more or less opposite St John's Church. A spendidly detailed interwar image gives a good idea of prices in those pre-inflation days.

**116** Further along Epping High Street, the drinking fountain can be seen on the left. This card is postmarked 1906 and, though its wide main street betrays a market town, the impression is still of a very quiet rural location.

**117** Local tradesmen's advertisements. The *White Swan*, which stood close to the *George and Dragon*, was demolished after the war.

**118** Pyne's drapery. A car waits outside Pyne's, one of Epping's best-loved shops, whose recent demise caused much soul-searching in the town about its long-term future as a shopping centre.

**19** *Right*. Williams' wine merchant. Unfortunately, whisky can no longer be purchased in Epping High Street at 17s. or 20s. a gallon.

**20** *Below left*. Cornwell's Bakery. Whatever happened to 'Scotch Oatmeal Bread manufactured from the best East Lothian Oatmeal'?

**21** *Below right*. Simpson's boot manufacturer. In the late Victorian period, Epping had a large number of boot and shoe makers. Of more interest perhaps is the smaller advertisement for Doye's taxidermy service. There was a big demand for skilled taxidermists from sportsmen and naturalists in the Epping Forest area, and as early as 1848 an Essex directory carried an advertisement for a professional 'bird-stuffer' in Epping.

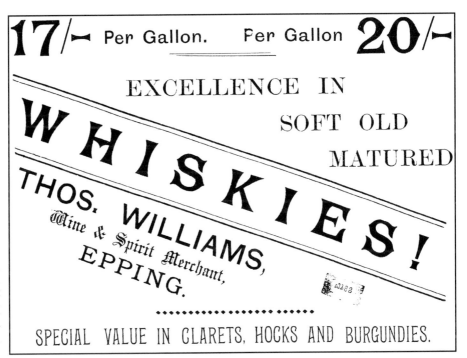

**122**  Epping High Street. The white-fronted building is the *Duke of York*, demolished in 1931 to make way for Barclay Bank. Cottis' bicycle shop is out of view on the right, while to the left is Guest's butcher, and beyond, the looming bulk of St John's.

**123**  Epping High Street. Squires can be seen again on the left in this charming view. Next to Squires is the wrought iron gateway leading to the Archimedean Iron Works; this was the Cottis family business and the town's largest employer.

**24**  Epping High Street. The gabled property at the centre of this view is Victoria Buildings, opened in 1899 and housing a large hall for public meetings on the upper floor. The Urban District Council met here, and there were lively political gatherings and social events too. The ground floor was occupied by the premises of Alfred Davis, an Epping printer prominent in public life; he produced a large number of local postcards, many of which have been used in this book. Victoria Buildings was one of the last commissions executed by the prominent Loughton architect Edmund Egan; the site is now occupied by the Co-op store.

**25**  Epping High Street, *c.*1960. The weatherboarded shop on the left is Batchelor's saddlery, and beyond is the *Black Dog*, since replaced by shops.

**126** Epping High Street. A mid-1960s view of the south side of the High Street; a range of roofscapes and shops old and new. The tall building with dormer windows is on the site of Clark's smithy, demolished in 1961. The building beyond that is on the site of the *White Lion*, also pulled down in the same year.

**127** At the north end of Epping High Street, the view opens outwards onto The Green, while behind the cameraman is Epping Plain, open land in the last century but now completely wooded. On the right is the Theydon Grove estate; the vast edifice and grounds were comprehensively redeveloped in the 1960s.

**28** Lindsey Street. Running from Epping Green to Epping Upland, Lindsey Street has retained some of the old-world tranquillity lost in the High Street. The area was formerly a melange of small cottages and local industries, one of which is still recalled in Maltings Lane.

**29** Hummerston's bakery. This advert from the *Epping & Ongar Almanack* dates from the turn of the century.

# G. HUMMERSTON,

## *Baker and Confectioner,*

### HIGH STREET, EPPING.

Best Bread and Flour only.   Brown Bread made to order.

#### FAMILIES WAITED UPON DAILY.

## TRY OUR SELF-RAISING FLOUR.

Hams, Tongues, and Bacon Smoked and Dried in a superior manner at

## G. HUMMERSTON'S Old-Established Bacon Stores,

### HIGH STREET, EPPING.

N.B.—Drying done for the Trade.

**30** *Above left.* Cottis' ironmongery. The first Cottis store, opened in the 1870s, is here seen proudly displaying a wide range of agricultural equipment. The Cottis family were the most prominent of Victorian Epping's many tradesmen, and for a time dominated political and social life. Church's butcher's shop is on the left.

**31** *Below left.* Cottis' hardware store. By the 1950s the ornate ironmongery had mutated into this rather more utilitarian hardware shop. The Cottis garage stands on the left, next to Barclays Bank. The company closed down in the 1960s.

**32** *Above.* Cottis' bicycle shop. This small weatherboarded shop was opened in a former bakery in 1896, and was the brainchild of Crispus Cottis, a well-known cycling champion. He later became the head of the Cottis concern and was a much-respected local tradesman and magistrate. At one stage, the company produced its own bicycle to his specification, the 'Archimedian'. In this view from *c.*1900, Crispus Cottis stands in the doorway of his shop with his derby hat tipped back rather casually on the back of his head.

**33** *Right.* Sworder's auctioneers, 1906. Sworder's occupied part of Victoria Buildings, already seen in an earlier photograph. The company held the franchise to act as auctioneers for Epping Market, which gave them considerable local prominence. Hugh Sworder and his partner Harry Knight are seen here standing outside their premises. Hugh Sworder died in 1921; the firm became Knight & Trotter, and was later taken over by the Loughton auctioneers Ambrose & Son.

**134** Ongar High Street. 'High Street Central' seems rather a grand description of this peaceful turn-of-the-century village scene, looking north. The vast red-brick bulk of the *Bull Hotel* dominates the west side of the road.

**135** Childs' drapery. A typical turn-of-the-century advert for Ongar's best-known local draper.

**36**  Ongar High Street. This 1906 view shows Budworth Hall, with its landmark clock-tower. The name commemorates
local landowner Captain P.J. Budworth, prominent in local politics and social life during the later Victorian period.

**37**  Smith's bakery. Smith's and
Mead's were the two best-known bakers
in Ongar at the turn of the century.

**138** Theydon Bois. These weatherboarded cottages were once part of Coppice Row, with Barnes the baker located in the nearest building. The cottages were demolished in the early 1970s after Essex County Council decided they were 'not worth preserving'. The postmark date is 1906, and the enigmatic message on the back reads: 'Dear Ettie, thanks for your kind remembrance, I trust you have forgiven me long ago ... I sincerely hope your face is better'!

**139** Oak Avenue, Theydon Bois. This fine prospect of oaks was planted on the green in 1832 by Robert Westley Hall Dare, lord of the manor of Theydon Bois.

**140** The Cross Roads, Theydon Bois. An idyllic rural scene.

**141** Piercing Hall, Theydon Bois. Looking back down towards the village. On Chapman and André's 1777 map of Essex, Piercing Hill was shown as Priors-horne Corner, and there does not seem to be any satisfactory explanation of the name.

**142** *Above*. Theydon Bois from Abridge Road. A more modern perspective, from the other side of the village, and dating from about 1960.

**143** *Below left*. Abridge, *c*.1912. Rebuilt in the mid-19th century, the *Blue Boar* dominates the curving row of buildings known as Market Place. A brewer's dray piled high with barrels stands outside the inn. The village grew up beside what was once a main road to London, some distance from the parish church and hall, which are located at Lambourne End.

**144** *Below*. Abridge, *c*.1908. Another view of the village, with the weatherboarded frontage and yard of Riggs Retreat on the right. One of the smaller of the many temperance refreshment establishments set up around the Forest by the Riggs family in the last century. The building housing Brighty's is early 16th-century.

**145** *Above.* Abridge, *c.*1934. A jaunty scene from the inter-war years. Children congregate outside Mrs. Brighty's well-known sweetshop, while cyclists pedal by on the road towards Romford. The ornate Victorian façade of the *Crown Hotel* can be seen beyond.

**146** *Left.* Abridge Cash Supply Stores. This photograph is unfortunately damaged and undated, but supplies a wealth of detail about lifestyles long-vanished in the village of Abridge.

**147** *Left.* Passingford Bridge. Lying in Stapleford Tawney parish, this bridge has for centuries been a vital link in the Essex road network. Nowadays overshadowed by the nearby M25, the bridge was once part of the main road from London to Ongar and beyond. This present bridge dates from 1785.

# Social Life

There has been an astonishingly active social life in the area as far back as detailed records go. Over time the rumbustious activities which bound rural communities together were replaced by more genteel fare; the hunt, the fair and seasonal celebrations such as horkey (harvest festival) gave way to vicarage tea party and village fete. The Victorian mania for self-improvement gave rise to a host of clubs and societies. In Epping, a 'Literary and Mechanics Institute' was formed in 1895 (and still thrives as the Hemnall Social Club). A guide to Epping for 1960-61 shows a still thriving social scene; there was a film society, a camera club, a Co-op choir, a Silver Band and a floral society, not to mention the Women's Institute, the Coopersale Institute and Allnutts Institute.

Meanwhile in Ongar, Henry Gibson had built a lecture hall and the Budworth Hall was completed in 1886. There was also a short-lived Ongar Mechanics' Institute and, in the Edwardian period, a mania for organised leisure; the town had an Agricultural Association, a Constitutional Association, a Horticultural Society, and a Reading and Recreation Society.

As can be seen from the following images, sport was also an important social glue. Hunting was for centuries an important part of rural life over much of our area, ranging from illicit poaching in the forest (where venison was known euphemistically as 'black mutton') to organised fox-hunting and deer-hunting. Epping Forest deer were driven almost to extinction in the early 19th century, and the annual Epping Hunt degenerated into a brutal travesty using captive deer released for the occasion. The second half of the 19th century saw the rise of organised sport such as football and cricket, and in the following pages we see images of cricket, cycle racing and its motorised counterpart, speedway. The fate of a cricket pitch was still able to cause controversy in the 1980s, when public pressure forced the re-instatement of the pitch on Bell Common after the M25 had been tunnelled beneath it.

Perhaps uniquely in Essex, the Epping Forest area has acted as an inland tourist resort, providing a lively social life for outsiders, notably East Enders; the forest was often regarded as their 'playground'; even Queen Victoria recorded in her diary after opening the Forest to the public in 1882, 'the Park has been given to the poor of the East End as a sort of recreation ground'. To this day a fine day in London brings throngs of visitors to the Forest, but the scale is hardly comparable with the veritable invasions which packed the chartered trains and filled the roads with horse-drawn conveyances of every kind at the close of the Victorian Age. The enormous scale of the 'Retreats'—temperance refreshment rooms and amusement parks rolled into one—is hard to realise. The natural aspect of the forest is much stressed today, but a century ago a visit to the forest was very much thought of as a beano, with donkey rides, coconut shies, and a good meat tea.

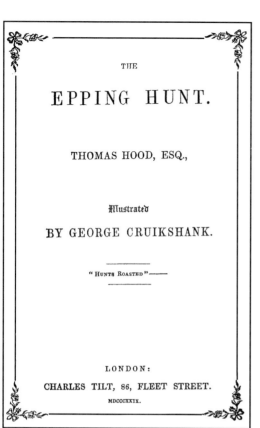

THE

# EPPING HUNT.

THOMAS HOOD, ESQ.,

Illustrated

BY GEORGE CRUIKSHANK.

———
"Hunts Roasted"———
———

LONDON:
CHARLES TILT, 86, FLEET STREET.
MDCCCXXIX.

**148** *Left*. The Epping Hunt. Until the early 19th century, the Epping Hunt was one of the forest's great social occasions. The Hunt began about 1226, the right supposedly granted to the citizens of London by Henry III to hunt in the forest on Easter Day. By 1827, however, there were no longer any red deer in the forest and very few fallow, and the hunt had degenerated into a cruel farce. A caged stag was carted around from inn to inn then released and killed before a baying mob. Thomas Hood's satirical poem *The Epping Hunt*, published in 1829, did much to hasten the end of the spectacle.

**149** *Below*. The Epping Hunt. Hood's poem mocked the drunken rowdiness which accompanied the hunt and, after publication, no more caged deer were released for slaughter, though the annual drinking binge and boisterous behaviour lingered on at various forest locations until about 1882, notably in the High Beach area. Hood was fortunate in securing the artistic skills of Cruickshank as illustrator for his poem.

**150** *Right*. Theydon Bois Cricket Club. Resplendent in the toppers, the members of Theydon Bois C.C. pause from their effort on the green to pose for the camera.

**151** *Below right*. Theydon Bois Football Club modelling the latest in leisurewear. The team was: (back row, left to right) W. Austin, Harold Parish, and 'Taff' Patience; (middle row, left to right) Tim Wood, Horace Morgan, Bert Gwilliam; (front row, left to right) Ernie Maynard, Sid Osborne, Jock Wiseman, Dick Thompson, and one Mr. Coates.

"When all at once he saw the beast
Come charging in his rear."

**152** Cycles outside Hummerston's Tea Rooms, Epping. In 1892, a cinder cycle track was laid down behind the *King's Oak* in High Beach, and the Essex Cycling Union held its race meets there, as did other cycling clubs. There was keen interest in local heroes such as the Essex-born Charlie Barden, who twice came second in the World Professional Championship (in 1896 and 1897), won various world records and was several times British national champion. Cycling remains a popular pastime in the Epping Forest area, particularly within the forest itself. Many tea rooms such as Hummerston's welcomed this passing trade, and this view shows numerous bikes parked outside in 1902, with members of the Hummerston family standing nearby.

**153** King's Oak Speedway Programme, 1928. Dirt-track motorcycle racing had its origins in America in 1902, with many of the rules evolved in Australia. Later known as speedway, it first came to Britain on 19 February 1928, at the Kings' Oak course. The sport caught on immediately, and by the 5 May programme, crowds of over 20,000 were gathering at High Beach to watch.

**154**  Riggs Retreat, Theydon Bois. Managed by Thomas Riggs, the Theydon Bois branch was opened in 1882 on the north side of Coppice Row, abutting Theydon Plain. In 1916 it was sold to Edwin Yates. It survived until 1940 when it was hit by a parachute mine which destroyed both Riggs and the rival Gray's Retreats and killed some soldiers billeted there.

**155**  The Tea Rooms, Riggs Retreat, Theydon Bois. Note the all-important tea-urn at the end of each table!

**156** *Above*. Roserville Retreat, High Beach. After the destruction of Riggs Retreat at Wellington Hill, William Rigg took over and expanded the Roserville (*sic*) Retreat next to the *King's Oak*. This had first been set up as the Rosherville Tea Gardens in 1883 (Rosherville was a former riverside resort near Gravesend very popular with East End trippers). Roserville survived in one form or another until 1959, though Riggs' interest in the site ended in 1926.

**157** *Above right*. Grand organ at the *King's Oak Hotel*. Places of entertainment in the forest went to extraordinary lengths to provide novelties for the fickle trippers!

**158** *Right*. High Street bunting, Epping. Epping loves a show, and here the Coronation of 1911 was a chance to put out the flags.

Grand Organ, King's Oak Hotel.
High Beech, Epping Forest.

**159** *Left*. Epping High Street, 27 May 1961. The Civic Trust's High Street Improvement Scheme was celebrated with a visit by the Lord Mayor of London and a carnival parade. Ironically the town's major facelift resulted in the demolition of several important historic buildings. Cottis' shop can be seen in the background; by 1961 it was no longer an ironmonger's store but sold electrical equipment.

**160** *Below left*. Crab apple seller. The cries of street-sellers now echo no more round our towns and villages; yet not so long ago the call of the muffin man and others were a welcome addition to the pattern of life. This unusual picture shows an elderly gent outside the *Wake Arms* selling strings of crab apples. Was this for jam-making or something more alcoholic?

**161** *Below*. An outing from Epping. The Sunday outing or 'Treat' was once a staple of social life. Here a group of Epping chaps are dressed in their Edwardian best and ready for a beano.

**162** The bellringers of All Saints', Epping Upland, are enjoying an excursion to Southend-on-Sea organised by Rev. W.A. Limbrick. The trip took place in about 1925, shortly after the opening of the Southend Arterial Road from Wanstead made charabanc trips much easier.

**163** Hunt meet at Matching Green. This part of Essex was once considered the best fox-hunting territory in th county.

**164** Epping Literary and Mechanics' Institute. Founded in 1895, the Institute, now the Hemnall Social Club, is still thriving.

# *Transport*

Historically, the area's road network essentially comprised a series of roads radiating out of London, like the spokes of a wheel, with cross-country routes joining them at various points. The road through Epping to Harlow and Bishop's Stortford and the Ongar road to Chelmsford were two of the most important, while to the south of our area was the Essex Great Road (now the A12), which followed the old Roman road from London to Colchester. The Roman road to Dunmow between Hobbs Cross and Toot Hill was still in use as part of the main London-Newmarket road until a road was cut through Epping Forest in the 17th century. A stagecoach ride through Epping Forest could be a hazardous business in the 18th century, as highwaymen plied their brutal trade. Dick Turpin was only the most notorious of these thugs. The condition of the roads themselves was also something of a gamble; Pepys commented on the poor state of the road through Epping Forest in 1659, and things did not improve much in the following two centuries. In such circumstances it was vital that bridges at least were kept in good repair, and the court records of Essex are full of disputes over such strategic crossings as Passingford Bridge and Ackingford Bridge.

The advent of railways put paid to coaching days. The Eastern Counties Railway reached Loughton via Woodford from Stratford in 1856, and was extended to Epping and Ongar in 1865. This line was important not only in the development of 'dormitory towns' for London but also for bringing huge numbers of trippers from the East End to Epping Forest. There were ambitious plans for further extensions of the railway network, the most controversial being the 1880s proposal to extend the Chingford line through the forest to High Beach. This was defeated after a storm of protest. The Central Essex Light Railway scheme of 1888 envisaged an extension of the Ongar line up the Roding valley as far as Sible Hedingham, and there were also proposals to link Ongar to Chelmsford via Writtle. A proposal to extend the Ongar line to Dunmow was aired as recently as 1960.

The Loughton to Ongar line became part of London Transport's Central Line following electrification as far as Epping on 25 September 1949; the Ongar extension had to wait until 1957 for electrification. Although an integral part of the county's transport network as seen through Essex eyes, from London Transport's point of view the Ongar extension was one of the system's furthest-flung outposts, and consequently ripe for run-down. The single track was never supplied with sufficient power to run more than two four-car trains at any one time.

The little halt at Blake Hall was closed in 1981, and the following year the Epping-Ongar branch became a peak hour shuttle service only. After a protracted battle and falling passenger numbers, the branch closed on 30 September 1994. There are, at the time of writing (1997), rival schemes to revive the line and run it as a private venture.

The military airfields in the area have in peacetime been turned to civilian, making the area something of a mecca for flight enthusiasts. The meteoric career of Edward

Hillman in the 1930s launched Stapleford Airfield as a short-lived international airport, and possibly the first and only airport with a flight timetable integrated into a region-wide coach network. Today it is home to Europe's busiest flying school, the Stapleford Flying Club. There was a short-lived 'Loughton Aerodrome' (not to be confused with Stapleford, also sometimes known as Loughton Aerodrome!) nearby at Abridge, on Piggott's Farm. At North Weald, the former R.A.F. base—which normally acts as the site of one of Essex's largest car boot fairs—revs up several times a year to the roar of fighter planes and memories are revived as vintage aircraft circle the runways and go through their manoeuvres.

More recently, the 'Great Car Society' announced by Mrs. Thatcher is certainly well catered for in this part of the world. The area is bisected north-south by the M11 (opened in 1977) and east-west by the M25 (opened in 1984); all our towns and villages are congested by ever-increasing traffic which is affecting the very rural charm which brings people to the area in the first place. There is obviously no easy answer to this issue!

**165**  *Below*. Epping to Ongar line. An Epping-bound train has just left North Weald on the Ongar line in 1929, during the golden age of the Ongar line. The Epping-Ongar extension opened in 1865 and survived until 1994, though with a much reduced shuttle service since 1982.

**166**  *Above right*. Epping to Ongar Line. G.E.R. locomotive No. 63 near Epping station, *c*.1911. The engine was a Class G69 2-4-2.

**167** The staff of Theydon Bois station straddle the track, *c.*1900. The opening of the station in 1865 transformed Theydon Bois, bringing it into relatively close contact with London and encouraging housing development.

**168** Stapleford Airfield. Opened in 1932 and variously known as 'London East Airport', 'Essex Airport', 'Abridge Aiport', 'Loughton Aerodrome' and 'Stapleford Abbots Airport', the airfield operated flights to Paris, Ostend, Brussels and Antwerp as well as several internal routes. This view shows a Hillman Airways de Havilland Dragon DH89 (G-ADEC). These dependable little planes were a familiar sight in Essex skies for many years; no less a pilot than Amy Johnson once flew them from Stapleford Airfield. Hillman Airways left Stapleford for Gatwick in 1935, and the company merged that year with two other airlines to form British Airways.

# War

The area covered by this book occupies an arc to the north-east of London and thus has been important to the defence of the capital at least since Napoleonic times. During the invasion scare of 1813, large camps were thrown up at Epping and other places across Essex, and a network of beacons built, one being sited at Ongar.

**169** First World War meat queue, Epping. Rationing during the First World War is much less well documented than its 1939-45 counterpart. This photograph is therefore a valuable piece of local social history. The queue stands outside Kirkby's butchers; note the heavily grilled window.

During the First World War air power first became a significant factor, and a series of aerodromes were hastily constructed to defeat the menace of bombing, first from Zeppelins, then from long-range Gotha bombers. In 1916, airfields came into operation at North Weald, Suttons Farm (Hornchurch), and Hainault Farm (Chadwell Heath), and there was considerable success in destroying the terrifying Zeppelins. The Gotha bombers came too late in the war to alter its course, but there were still furious dogfights over Essex skies in the spring and summer of 1917 and 1918. The war memorials sprinkled across the area are testimony to those men—some little more than boys—and women of the area who still lie in Flanders fields. The memorials are various: in Fyfield, the parish church has a memorial window; there is a churchyard octagonal column and two oak screens in the nave at Epping Upland Church; a granite Celtic cross at Matching lists 20 dead; an Ionic cross at Theydon Bois lists 27 dead, and the cross at Epping records 96 names.

In 1939-45, civilians were truly brought into the war, and the 'Home Front' became as important as military operations overseas. There were vast preparations for invasion. An 'Outer London Defence Ring' was constructed—roughly along the present route of the M25—comprising anti-tank ditches and barriers, road blocks and pill-boxes. The route extended from the Lea at Nazeing, across to Perry Hill, down through Bumble's Green, Epping Upland and to Copped Hall. The defences then cut right through Epping Forest to Debden Green, across to Rolls Park at Chigwell, on to Chigwell Row, into Redbridge and southwards to the Thames.

The Epping Forest area formed an intermediate evacuation zone for East Enders and, for the duration, was also promoted as an area for quiet country breaks. An area at Upshire was formed into a vast rest camp for exhausted East End fire crews. There was pretty indiscriminate bombing across the whole area during the Battle of Britain, and it came under fire again during the V-1 and V-2 rocket offensive of 1944. The second V-2 to hit England struck near Epping on 7 September 1944.

**170** Epping War Memorial. Dedicated on 8 May 1920, this memorial on Long Green commemorated the 66 men of Epping who fell in the First World War; more names were added after the 1939-45 conflict. Almost every village lost some of its sons, and this monument is just one of many, some humble, some grand, across the Epping and Ongar area.

The airfields of the area were front-line bases; 151 Squadron moved to Stapleford in August 1940 and saw action immediately. 111 Squadron had already moved to North Weald in May of that year. North Weald and the associated Operations Room at Blake Hall (now fortunately preserved as a museum) saw a large number of 'refugee' pilots operating from its runways, including Norwegians, Poles and Czechs. One unfortunate tragedy nowadays known as 'friendly fire' occurred early in the war. Pilots from 56 Squadron, based at North Weald, were attacked by Spitfires from Hornchurch in September 1939; one pilot was shot down and killed in what became known as 'The Battle of Barking Creek'. The first Eagle Squadron—American pilots serving in the R.A.F. before America joined the war in 1941—was also based at North Weald.

At the end of the war Hill Hall was for a short time (1945-48) converted from its earlier role as a D-Day transit camp to a prisoner-of-war camp. Epping, Ongar and other smaller towns and villages celebrated the end of the war with street parties, bonfires, victory parades and, most of all, a vast sense of relief.

# Index

Roman numerals refer to text pages and arabic numerals to individual illustrations